The Abrahamic Promises in Galatians

A. Blake White

Books by A. Blake White

The Newness of the New Covenant

The Law of Christ: A Theological Proposal

Galatians: A Theological Interpretation

Abide in Him:
A Theological Interpretation of John's First Letter

Union with Christ: Last Adam & Seed of Abraham

What is New Covenant Theology? An Introduction

Theological Foundations for New Covenant Ethics

Missional Ecclesiology

The Abrahamic Promises in Galatians

A. Blake White

5317 Wye Creek Drive, Frederick, MD 21703-6938
301-473-8781 | info@newcovenantmedia.com
www.NewCovenantMedia.com

The Abrahamic Promises in Galatians

To my brother, Aaron White
Proud of you, bro.
I admire your "pure religion." Much love!

Table of Contents

Introduction

I love the book of Galatians. Careful study of this blessed letter is deeply rewarding and I am grateful to have had the opportunity to present this material at the 2012 Providence Theological Seminary Doctrinal Conference in Colorado Springs, Colorado, and the annual John Bunyan Conference in 2013, hosted in Lewisburg, Pennsylvania. This topic has intrigued many for a while so I am also grateful for an opportunity to expound it. This book is an expansion of chapters 9-11 of my *Union with Christ: Last Adam and Seed of Abraham.*

New Covenant Theology often preaches about the importance of letting the apostles teach us how to approach the Old Testament. This is right and good, but we also need to demonstrate it from text after text. This little book is offered to that end with one set of important Old Testament promises examined in one letter of the New Testament. I hope and pray it is illuminating.

Chapter 1:
The Abrahamic Promise in Genesis 12:1-3

The Story So Far:

The first chapters of the Bible are familiar to us all. Genesis 1-2 is wonderful, but chapters 3-11 are bleak. First came Adam's fall, then Noah's, then the city builders'. Babel, in essence, was about human achievement. They wanted to make a name for themselves by building a tower with its top in the heavens. They thought they were reaching the heavens, but – note the irony - God *still* had to come down (Gen 11:7). The "great name" the builders strove for is *given* to Abram (Gen 11:4, 12:2). With all the blatant rebellion, chapter 11 leaves us with the question, "Is God finished with the nations? Has his patience run out?"Genesis 12 is God's response.[1] Christopher Wright, in his superb book *The Mission of God*, writes,

> What can God do next? Something that only God could have thought of. He sees an elderly, childless couple in the land of Babel and decides to make them the fountain head, the launch pad of his whole mission of cosmic redemption. We can almost hear the sharp intake of breath among the heavenly hosts when the astonishing plan was revealed. They knew, as the reader of Genesis 1-11 now knows, the sheer scale of devastation that serpentine evil and human recalcitrance have

---

[1] William J. Dumbrell, *Search for Order* (Eugene, OR: Wipf and Stock, 1994), 34.

wrought in God's creation. What sort of an answer can be provided through Abram and Sarai? Yet that is precisely the scale of what now follows. The call of Abram is the beginning of God's answer to the evil of human hearts, the strife of nations and the groaning brokenness of his whole creation. A new world, ultimately a new creation, begins in this text. But it is a new world that bursts out of the womb of the old – the old world portrayed in Genesis 1-11.[2]

Genesis 12 serves as a transitional passage – from Adam to Abraham. It brings about a new phase of history.[3] As Wright notes, a new creation emerges here.[4] That's why in Romans 4:17, when describing the promise to Abraham, Paul speaks of God as the one "who gives life to the dead and calls into existence the things that do not exist."[5] Genesis 12 is a reiteration in new form of the original promise given in Genesis 3:15.[6] A rabbinic midrash on Genesis has

---

[2] Christopher J.H. Wright, *The Mission of God* (Downers Grove, IL: IVP Academic, 2006), 199-200.

[3] William J. Dumbrell, *Covenant and Creation* (Carlisle, PA: Paternoster, 1984), 58; T. Desmond Alexander, *From Paradise to the Promised Land* (Grand Rapids: Baker Academic, 2002), 145.

[4] Wright, *The Mission of God,* 199; Dumbrell, *Covenant and Creation,* 63; Andreas J. Köstenberger and Peter T. O'Brien, *Salvation to the Ends of the Earth* (Downers Grove, IL: IVP, 2001), 28.

[5] Stephen J. Wellum, "Baptism and the Relationship Between the Covenants," in *Believer's Baptism: Sign of the New Covenant in Christ* eds. Thomas R. Schreiner and Shawn D. Wright (Nashville: B&H Academic, 2006), 130; Peter J. Gentry and Stephen J. Wellum, *Kingdom Through Covenant: A Biblical-Theological Understanding of the Covenants* (Wheaton, IL: Crossway Books, 2012), 225.

[6] James Hamilton, "The Seed of the Woman and the Blessing of Abraham," *Tyndale Bulletin* 58.2 (2007); Michael W. Goheen, *A Light to the Nations* (Grand Rapids: Baker, 2011), 28.

God say, "I will make Adam first and if he goes astray I will send Abraham to sort it out."[7] Similarly, N.T. Wright notes, "Abraham emerges within the structure of Genesis as the answer to the plight of all humankind. The line of disaster and of the 'curse,' from Adam, through Cain, through the Flood to Babel, begins to be reversed when God calls Abraham and says, 'in you shall all the families of the earth be blessed'."[8]

Genesis 12:1-3 reads, "Now the LORD said to Abram, 'Go from your country and your kindred and your father's house to the land that I will show you. And I will make of you a great nation, and I will bless you and make your name great, so that you will be a blessing. I will bless those who bless you, and him who dishonors you I will curse, and in you all the families of the earth shall be blessed'."

---

[7] *Gen. Rab.* 14:6 quoted in Goheen, *A Light to the Nations,* 27.

[8] N.T. Wright, *The New Testament and the People of God* (Minneapolis: Fortress, 1992), 262; Similarly, Stephen Dempster writes, "God's programme [*sic*] with and through Abraham is to restore the original conditions of creation described in Genesis 1-2," in *Dominion and Dynasty: A Theology of the Hebrew Bible* (Downers Grove, IL: InterVarsity Press, 2003), 79. Craig A. Blaising and Darrel L. Bock also write, "Like the Noahic covenant, the Abrahamic covenant stands in contrast to the judgments of God on human sin and presents anew the plan of creation," in *Progressive Dispensationalism* (Grand Rapids: Baker, 1993), 130.

Chapter 2:
The Structure of Genesis 12:1-3

It is helpful to see the structure of these verses. There are two imperatives followed by three promises, with the first set to Abraham and second set to the world in relationship to Abraham:

I. Go to the land I will show you.

    A. I will make you into a great nation[9]

    B. I will bless you

    C. I will make your name great

II. Be a blessing.[10]

    A. I will bless those who bless you

    B. I will curse whoever curses you

    C. All peoples will be blessed through you[11]

---

[9] The command, "Be fruitful" has turned into a promise: "I will make your fruitful" (Wright, *The New Testament and the People of God*, 263.). The word for "nation" is *goy* which is usually reserved for the world community excluding Israel; when used of Israel it is often used in a pejorative manner (cf. Jud 2:20). The normal way of referring to Israel is *am*. This usage is probably to point to the later emergence of Israel as a geopolitical entity. See W. J. Dumbrell, "The Covenant With Abraham," *The Reformed Theological Review* 41.2 (May-August 1982), 43; Paul R. Williamson, *Sealed With an Oath* (Downers Grove, IL: IVP, 2007), 82-83; Alexander, *From Paradise to the Promised Land* 144.

[10] Our English translations often translate this phrase as "and you will be a blessing." This is a fine translation but the fact that it is an imperative is often missed. I prefer, "and you, be a blessing." See Christopher Wright, *The Mission of God,* 200-01.

Here we have two goals: 1) to form Abraham into a great nation with land, offspring, and blessing, and 2) to bless all nations through Abraham's one great nation.[12] The final clause, "all peoples on earth will be blessed through you," is the principal statement of these verses.[13] As Christopher Wright says, "Blessing for the nations is the bottom line, textually and theologically, of God's promise to Abraham."[14] So we have a two-fold agenda here: Abraham and his family are first of all the recipients of blessing, and then they are the mediators of blessing. They are blessed in order to be a blessing.[15] The nature of this blessing is not fully unpacked

---

[11] Wright, *The Mission of God,* 200-01; so also Gentry and Wellum, *Kingdom Through Covenant,* 234.

[12] Williamson, *Sealed With An Oath,* 79, 82.

[13] Goheen, *A Light to the Nations,* 30-31.

[14] Wright, *The Mission of God*, 194.

[15] The missiological implications of these verses are *many*. The mission of God starts here. As Christopher Wright observes, "We cannot speak biblically of the doctrine of election without insisting that it was never an end in itself but a means to the greater end of the ingathering of the nations. Election must be seen as missiological, not merely soteriological," in *The Mission of God,* 369. Michael Goheen continues, "Abraham's particular election is the instrument for the universal purpose of God with the whole world. Thus in the biblical story, privilege and responsibility, salvation and service, receiving, and mediating blessing, belong together in election. God's people are a *so that people:* they are chosen *so that* they might know God's salvation and then invite all nations into it," in *A Light to the Nations,* 31. The Great Commission can be seen as a christological mutation of the original Abrahamic commission: "Go ... and be a blessing ... and all nations on earth will be blessed through you," Wright, *The Mission of God,* 213. See my *Missional Ecclesiology* (Frederick, MD: New Covenant Media).

here in Genesis, but as revelation progresses its nature is clarified.[16]

It is hard to overestimate the importance of these promises *for everything.* "Abraham is where it all starts. Abraham is where things get shaped."[17] This chapter is the basis for all of God's dealings with mankind. Here we have the "theological blueprint for the redemptive history of the world."[18] Here we have the Bible's Magna Carta![19] This is the foundation for God's "single-plan-through-Israel-for-the-world."[20] Darrell Bock and Craig Blaising write, "The Abrahamic covenant consequently sets forth the foundational relationship between God and all humankind from Abraham onward. This means that to understand the Bible, one must read it in view of the Abrahamic covenant, for that covenant with Abraham is the foundational framework for interpreting the Scripture and the history of redemption which it reveals."[21]

---

[16] Craig A. Blaising and Darrell L. Bock, *Progressive Dispensationalism* (Grand Rapids: Baker Books, 2000), 140.

[17] N.T. Wright, *Justification* (Downers Grove, IL: IVP, 2009), 217.

[18] Dumbrell, "The Covenant With Abraham," 46; idem., *Covenant and Creation,* 66; Williamson similarly notes, "These three verses fix the agenda not only for the patriarchal narratives, but also for the rest of the Pentateuch and beyond. Therefore, this divine speech to Abram is one of the most important revelations in the whole of Scripture," in *Sealed With an Oath,* 77.

[19] Williamson, *Sealed With an Oath,* 77.

[20] Wright, *Justification,* 216.

[21] Blaising and Bock, *Progressive Dispensationalism,* 135; see also 172; Stephen J. Wellum agrees, writing, "Scripture presents the Abrahamic covenant as the basis for all God's dealings with the human race and the backbone for understanding the biblical covenants. Truly, it is through Abraham and his seed—ultimately viewed in terms of our

As Paul would say much later, here we have the gospel in advance (Gal 3:8).

This promise is *the* basic promise of the Bible. All other promises are expansions of this one.[22] The Mosaic covenant was built off of this one (Exod 2:24, 6:4-5). Genesis 12:2-3 is reiterated in a new form in Exodus 19:4-6: "You yourselves have seen what I did to the Egyptians, and how I bore you on eagles' wings and brought you to myself. Now therefore, if you will indeed obey my voice and keep my covenant, you shall be my treasured possession among all peoples, for all the earth is mine; and you shall be to me a kingdom of priests and a holy nation. These are the words that you shall speak to the people of Israel."

There are three main elements promised: land, offspring, and blessing (or a special relationship with God).[23] The Da-

---

Lord Jesus Christ (Gal 3:16)—that our triune God fulfills his eternal purpose and promise to save a people for himself and to usher in a new creation. This is borne out, not only in terms of OT theology, but also in how the NT authors interpret the fulfillment of the Abrahamic promise in light of the person and work of Christ (e.g., Romans 4 and Galatians 3)," in his programmatic essay "Baptism and the Relationship Between the Covenants," 128-29, 132; Also see Kostenberger and O'Brien, *Salvation to the Ends of the Earth,* 32, 252; David Baker, *Two Testaments, One Bible* (Downers Grove, IL: IVP Academic, 2010), 242.

[22] Baker, *Two Testaments, One Bible*, 202-03.

[23] Baker, *Two Testaments, One Bible*, 203. The relationship is begun and the promises given in chapter 12. The covenant is formalized in chapter 15, and confirmed in chapter 17. T.D. Alexander and his student Paul Williamson see a "new" covenant in Genesis 17. As William J. Dumbrell notes, the sense in chapter 17 is that of setting into operation the earlier covenant promises of Genesis 15, in "Abraham and the Abrahamic covenant in Galatians 3:1-14," in *The Gospel to the Nations: Perspectives on Paul's Mission,* eds. Peter Bolt and Mark Thompson

vidic covenant is a reiteration of the Abrahamic. David is promised *blessing*. Second Samuel 7:9 reads, "And I have been with you wherever you went and have cut off all your enemies from before you." Second Samuel 7:14-15 read, "I will be to him a father, and he shall be to me a son. When he commits iniquity, I will discipline him with the rod of men, with the stripes of the sons of men, but my steadfast love will not depart from him, as I took it from Saul, whom I put away from before you" (see 7:23-24 as well). David is promised *land:* "And I will appoint a place for my people Israel and will plant them, so that they may dwell in their own place and be disturbed no more" (2 Sam 7:10). Like Abraham, he is also promised *offspring*: "Moreover, the LORD declares to you that the LORD will make you a house. When your days are fulfilled and you lie down with your fathers, I will raise up your offspring after you, who shall come from your body, and I will establish his kingdom."[24]

(Downers Grove, IL: IVP, 2000), 31. Gentry and Wellum write, "We might compare the relationship between God and Abraham to a marriage. The giving of the promises in chapter 12 would then represent the betrothal or engagement. The covenant making in chapter 15 and confirmation in chapter 17 would correspond to the wedding vows of the marriage covenant. After testing Abraham, God reiterates his promises by a might oath," in *Kingdom Through Covenant,* 230.

[24] Baker, *Two Testaments, One Bible,* 206.

Chapter 3:
The Abrahamic Promises in the Letter to the Galatians

Galatians 3:1-16 says,

O foolish Galatians! Who has bewitched you? It was before your eyes that Jesus Christ was publicly portrayed as crucified. Let me ask you only this: Did you receive the Spirit by works of the law or by hearing with faith? Are you so foolish? Having begun by the Spirit, are you now being perfected by the flesh? Did you suffer so many things in vain--if indeed it was in vain? Does he who supplies the Spirit to you and works miracles among you do so by works of the law, or by hearing with faith-- just as Abraham "believed God, and it was counted to him as righteousness"? Know then that it is those of faith who are the sons of Abraham. And the Scripture, foreseeing that God would justify the Gentiles by faith, preached the gospel before-hand to Abraham, saying, "In you shall all the nations be blessed." So then, those who are of faith are blessed along with Abraham, the man of faith. For all who rely on works of the law are under a curse; for it is written, "Cursed be everyone who does not abide by all things written in the Book of the Law, and do them." Now it is evident that no one is justified before God by the law, for "The righteous shall live by faith." But the law is not of faith, rather "The one who does them shall live by them." Christ redeemed us from the curse of the law by becoming a curse for us--for it is written, "Cursed is everyone who is hanged on a tree" - so that in Christ Jesus the blessing of Abraham might come to the Gentiles, so that we might receive the promised Spirit through faith. To give a human example, brothers: even with a man-made covenant, no one annuls it or adds to it once it has been ratified. Now the promises were made to Abraham and to his off-

spring. It does not say, "And to offsprings," referring to many, but referring to one, "And to your offspring," who is Christ.

I want to put my cards on the table. Before we look at how Paul, under the inspiration of the Holy Spirit, applies the Abrahamic promises, I want my presuppositions to be clear. I take 2 Corinthians 1:20 *literally:* "For no matter how many promises God has made, they are "Yes" in Christ." (NIV). I am advocating a "Christotelic" hermeneutic. Peter Enns notes, "To read the OT 'Christotelicly' is to read it *already knowing* that Christ is somehow the *end* (*telos*) to which the OT story is heading; in other words, to read the OT in light of the exclamation point of the history of revelation, the death and resurrection of Christ."[25] The New Testament provides God-breathed commentary on what the Old Testament means. We must interpret the Old Testament as Christian disciples. For Christian interpreters, we cannot approach the Old Testament as if the New Testament had not been written.[26] As Hans K. LaRondelle writes,

---

[25] Peter Enns, "Fuller Meaning, Single Goal: A Christotelic Approach to the New Testament Use of the Old in Its First-Century Interpretive Environment," in *Three Views on the New Testament Use of the Old Testament* eds. Kenneth Berding and Jonathan Lunde (Grand Rapids: Zondervan, 2007), 214; Idem., *Inspiration and Incarnation: Evangelicals and the Problem of the Old Testament* (Grand Rapids: Baker, 2005), 154; J.R. Daniel Kirk, *Jesus Have I Loved, but Paul?* (Grand Rapids: Baker Academic, 2011), 194-95; Dennis E. Johnson, *Him We Proclaim* (Phillipsburg, NJ: P&R, 2007) 140 n.14, 149; Graeme Goldsworthy, *Gospel-Centered Hermeneutics* (Downers Grove, IL: IVP Academic, 2006), 62-63.

[26] P.W.L. Walker, *Jesus and the Holy City* (Grand Rapids: Eerdmans, 1996), 313. Hans K. LaRondelle writes, "Christ alone is the true Interpreter of Israel's sacred Scriptures," *The Israel of God in Prophecy* (Berrien

The Christian understanding of the Old Testament is determined by the Christocentric focus by which the New Testament writers interpreted the Hebrew Scriptures ... The key to the Old Testament is not a rationalistic method or principle, be it literalism or allegorism, but Christ Jesus, the Son of God, as revealed in the New Testament. The Christian interpreter of the Old Testament is once and for all obliged to read the Hebrew Scriptures in the light of the New Testament as a whole, because the Old is interpreted authoritatively, under divine inspiration, in the New Testament as God's continuous history of salvation.[27]

The New Testament writers teach us about Jesus and the new covenant, but also about Genesis. Jesus says, "For if you believed Moses, you would believe me; for he wrote of me" (John 5:46).[28] Luke records how King Jesus gave the disciples on the road to Emmaus a lesson in Christotelic hermeneutics. As one New Testament scholar notes, "Luke explicitly attributes the origin of christological interpretation of the Old Testament to Jesus himself. From the retrospective

---

Springs, MI: Andrews University Press, 1983), 3 (cf. 1, 8, 14, 19, 23, 60).

[27] LaRondelle, *The Israel of God in Prophecy,* 8, 19.

[28] Contra Baker, who writes, "It is sometimes thought that the key to interpreting the Old Testament is in New Testament use of the Old. However, we live in a different world from the authors of the New Testament, and our task is not to imitate the way they interpreted the Old Testament but to develop our own way. Their methods of interpretation were suited to the needs of the first century, but cannot simply be repeated at the beginning of the twenty-first century. We can learn a great deal from the way early Christians read and understood the Old Testament, but to truly understand and respond to the Word of God today we should use the methods of modern hermeneutics," in *Two Testaments, One Bible,* 278.

standpoint of the resurrection, Luke insists that the whole story of Israel's Bible in all its parts was, in some mysterious manner, really 'about' Jesus. The concluding chapter of this gospel, therefore, encourages the reader to undertake a comprehensive reading of Israel's scripture in light of the story of Jesus to see how this claim might be true."[29]

Having shown my cards, let's recall the context of Galatians. The Abraham narrative would have been utilized by the Judaizers. We will take a brief look at each of the three principle promises of the Abrahamic covenant: offspring, blessing, and land. As we will see, land and offspring (as well as Sabbath and baptism) are great test cases for biblical theology (i.e., how one puts the canon together will be determinative for one's view of these issues).

---

[29] Richard B. Hays, "The Canonical Matrix of the Gospels," in *The Cambridge Companion to the Gospels* ed. Stephen C. Barton (Cambridge: Cambridge University Press, 2006), 69-70. Hays continues, "For Luke, then, the canonical matrix of Israel's Scripture is not merely a web of tales and images from which proof-texts may be selected at random; rather, for Luke the canonical matrix has a *plot*, and the gospel constitutes that plot's resolution. We understand the gospel rightly only when we see it as the outworking of God's purpose in history." "The Canonical Matrix of the Gospels," 70.

Chapter 4:
Offspring[30]

As has been pointed out, there are four senses of the offspring of Abraham found in Scripture:

1. Physical
2. Physical/Special
3. Christological
4. Ecclesial[31]

The key to understanding Paul's reworking of the offspring of Abraham is found in Galatians 3:16: "Now the promises were made to Abraham and to his offspring. It does not say, 'And to offsprings,' referring to many, but referring to one, 'And to your offspring,' who is Christ." This is the christological aspect of Abraham's offspring. Here, "offspring" is singular in form but is a collective noun and therefore can

---

[30] On this issue, see Wright, *Mission of God,* 343, 353, 455, 489, 528; N.T. Wright, *Justification* (Downers Grove, IL: IVP Academic, 2009), 142-43; E. Earl Ellis, *Paul's Use of the Old Testament* (Eugene, OR: Wipf and Stock, 1981), 136-37; William J. Dumbrell, "Abraham and the Abrahamic Covenant in Galatians 3:1-14," in *The Gospel to the Nations: Perspectives on Paul's Mission,* eds. Peter Bolt and Mark Thompson (Downers Grove, IL: IVP, 2000), 26, 27; Thomas R. Schreiner, *Galatians,* ZEC (Grand Rapids: Zondvervan, 2010), 57-58, 99, 130, 382, 399; LaRondelle, *The Israel of God,* 98-123.

[31] John G. Reisinger, *Abraham's Four Seeds* (Frederick, MD: New Covenant Media, 1998); Stephen J. Wellum, "Baptism and the Relationship Between the Covenants," 133-35; Gentry and Wellum, *Kingdom Through Covenant,* 115, 632, 696.

either be singular or plural in meaning (like our "fish" or "sheep") and Paul finds this significant. Christ is *the* offspring of Abraham in a unique sense.

Paul's interpretation is legitimate since it depends on 2 Samuel 7:12-14, where there is mention of a singular seed:[32] "When your days are fulfilled and you lie down with your fathers, I will raise up your *offspring* after you, *who* shall come from your body, and I will establish *his* kingdom. *He* shall build a house for my name, and I will establish the throne of *his* kingdom forever. I will be to *him* a father, and *he* shall be to me a son. When *he* commits iniquity, I will discipline *him* with the rod of men, with the stripes of the sons of men" (emphasis mine).

Back in Genesis 17:6, Abraham was promised that "kings shall come from you" (cf. also Gen 17:16, 35:11).[33] David was this offspring of Abraham and his greater Son is Jesus – the Messiah who is a corporate head over his people.[34] He is *the* offspring of Abraham. Speaking of the Davidic King of Israel, Psalm 72:17 says that people will be blessed in *him* and all nations will call *him* blessed.[35] As Richard Hays notes, "Paul's understanding of Jesus Christ as the one true heir of the promise to Abraham is the essential theological presupposition for his hermeneutical strategies."[36]

---

[32] Richard B. Hays, *Echoes of Scripture in the Letters of Paul* (London: Yale University Press, 1989), 85.

[33] See Daniel S. Diffey, "The Royal Promise in Genesis: The Often Underestimated Importance of Genesis 17:6, 17:16, and 35:11," *Tyndale Bulletin* 62.2 (2011), 313-16.

[34] Schreiner, *Galatians,* 229.

[35] Gentry and Wellum, *Kingdom Through Covenant,* 288-89.

[36] Hays, *Echoes of Scripture in the Letters of Paul,* 121.

Luke's record of Mary's song of praise confirms this. When Mary hears that she will bear the Son of the Most High who will be given the throne of *David* to reign forever, she concludes her song of praise with the following words: "He has helped his servant Israel, in remembrance of his mercy, as he spoke to our fathers, to Abraham and to his off-spring forever" (Luke 1:54-55).[37] It is confirmed further in Zechariah's prophecy:

> And his father Zechariah was filled with the Holy Spirit and prophesied, saying, "Blessed be the Lord God of Israel, for he has visited and redeemed his people and has raised up a horn of salvation for us in the house of his servant David, as he spoke by the mouth of his holy prophets from of old, that we should be saved from our enemies and from the hand of all who hate us; to show the mercy promised to our fathers and to remember his holy covenant, the oath that he swore to our father Abraham, to grant us that we, being delivered from the hand of our enemies, might serve him without fear, in holiness and righteousness before him all our days" (Luke 1:67-75).

Jesus is the offspring of David who brings the blessing of Abraham.[38]

The promises to Israel were conditional and Jesus, the Son of Abraham and David (Matt 1:1) is the only faithful Israel-ite. All of God's promises find their YES in him (2 Cor 1:20).

---

[37] Blaising and Bock write, "Mary's song reveals her belief that the one whom she would bear to fulfill the promises to David would also ful-fill the promises made to Abraham. In her mind the fulfillment of the Davidic covenant was the means by which the Abrahamic promise would be accomplished." *Progressive Dispensationalism,* 188.

[38] James Hamilton, "The Seed of the Woman and the Blessing of Abra-ham," *Tyndale Bulletin* 58.2 (2007), 271; Kirk, *Jesus Have I Loved, but Paul?,* 14-15; Note also that in Acts 3:24-26 it is the Servant of Isaiah who brings about the blessing of Abraham.

It is worth quoting Southern Baptist theologian Russell Moore at length on this point:

> For the new covenant apostles, Jew-Gentile unity is pivotal to the early church. It is about more than human relational harmony. Instead, it acknowledges that God's kingdom purposes are *in Christ*. He is the last man and the true Israel, the bearer of the Spirit. A Jewish person who clings to the tribal markings of the old covenant acts as though the eschaton has not arrived, as though one were still waiting for the promised seed. Both Jews and Gentiles must instead see their identities not in themselves or in the flesh but in Jesus Christ and in him alone. Jesus is the descendant of Abraham, the one who deserves the throne of David. He is the obedient Israel who inherits the blessings of the Mosaic covenant. He is the propitiation of God's wrath. He is the firstborn from the dead, the resurrection and the life. Those who are in Christ – whether Jew or Gentile – receive with him all the eschatological blessings that are due to him. In him, they are all, whether Jew or Gentile, sons of God – not only in terms of relationship with the Father but also in terms of promised inheritance (Rom 8:12-17). In Christ, they all – whether Jew or Gentile – are sons of Abraham, the true circumcision, the holy nation, and the household and commonwealth of God (Gal 3:23-4:7; Eph 2-3; Col 2:6-15; 3:3-11; 1 Pet 2:9-10).… Both Covenant Theology and Dispensationalism, however, often discuss Israel and the church without taking into account the christocentric nature of biblical eschatology. The future restoration of Israel has *never* been promised to the unfaithful, unregenerate members of the nation (John 3:3-10; Rom 2:25-29) – only to the faithful remnant. The church is not Israel, at least not in a direct, unmediated sense. The remnant of Israel – a biological descendant of Abraham, a circumcised Jewish firstborn son who is approved of by God for his obedience to the covenant – receives *all* of the promises due to him. Israel is Jesus of Nazareth, who, as promised to Israel,

is raised from the dead and marked out with the Spirit (Ezek 37:13-14; Rom 1:2-4)... Dispensationalists are right that only ethnic Jews receive the promised future restoration, but Paul makes clear that the "seed of Abraham" is singular, not plural (Gal 3:16). Only the circumcised can inherit the promised future for Israel. All believers – Jew and Greek, slave and free, male and female – are forensically Jewish firstborn sons of God (Gal 3:28). They are *in Christ*... In Christ, I inherit all the promises due to Abraham's offspring so that everything that is true of him is true of me... The future of Israel then does belong to Gentile believers but only because they are in union with a Jewish Messiah.[39]

Paul clearly realizes that Abraham's offspring includes a collective sense as well. He himself does this in this same chapter:

Galatians 3:7 - *"Know then that it is those of faith who are the sons of Abraham."*

Galatians 3:26-29 - *"for in Christ Jesus you are all sons of God, through faith. For as many of you as were baptized into Christ have put on Christ. There is neither Jew nor Greek, there is neither slave nor free, there is no male and female, for you are all one in Christ Jesus. And if you are Christ's, then you are Abraham's offspring, heirs according to promise."*

In Galatians 3:29 the "you" is plural (*humeis*). A good Texan translation would be "And if y'all are Christ's, then y'all are Abraham's offspring." Paul had a christocentric *and*

---

[39] Russell Moore, "Personal and Cosmic Eschatology," in *Theology for the Church*, ed. Daniel L. Akin (Nashville: B&H Academic, 2007), 867-68, 906-07; LaRondelle, *The Israel of God*, 64, 65, 68; Wellum, "Baptism and the Relationship Between the Covenants," 136.

an ecclesiocentric hermeneutic.[40] LaRondelle writes, "In biblical typology it is not Christ alone who is the antitype but *Christ and His people,* united in an unbreakable, organic unity, in God's saving purpose for the world."[41] This makes sense since "seed" reproduces in kind. Many seed can come from one seed.[42]

So we can ask, is Abraham's offspring Jesus or the church? Yes! The church inherits the promises made to Abraham by being in Christ.[43] Union with Christ is central in understanding the relationship between Israel and the church.[44]

This is the ecclesial sense of Abraham's offspring mentioned above, and is something that Covenant Theology tends to miss.[45] For example, Reformed Theologian Louis Berkhof states that the Abrahamic covenant is primarily spiritual and "is essentially identical with the 'new covenant' of the present dispensation."[46] He argues that since infants were included in the old dispensation as an integral

---

[40] See Hays, *Echoes of Scripture in the Letters of Paul,* 84-121; Kirk, *Jesus Have I Loved, but Paul?,* 63.

[41] LaRondelle, *The Israel of God,* 52.

[42] Blaising and Bock, *Progressive Dispensationalism,* 190.

[43] Donaldson, "The Kingdom of God and the Land," in *The Gospel and the Land of Promise,* 67.

[44] See my *Union With Christ: Last Adam and Seed of Abraham* (Frederick, MD: New Covenant Media, 2012), 55-62; Gentry and Wellum, *Kingdom Through Covenant,* 121-22, 690.

[45] For a devastating critique of Covenant Theology, see Stephen J. Wellum's essay, "Baptism and the Relationship Between the Covenants."

[46] Louis Berkhof, *Systematic Theology* (Grand Rapids: Eerdmans, 1996), 633.

part of the people of God, they should not be excluded from the new covenant community. Again, he writes, "Such an exclusion would seem to require a very explicit statement to that effect… if children received the sign and seal of the covenant in the old dispensation, the presumption is that they surely have a right to receive it in the new."[47] In other words, since in the old era Abraham and his offspring were to receive the sign of the covenant, so in the new believers and their offspring should receive the sign (hence infant baptism).

In my humble opinion, Berkhof and those of his theological persuasion miss the newness that the new covenant brings. Christ is the Mediator of the new covenant, which is the fulfillment of the Abrahamic covenant. Jesus as the final covenant Mediator brings *significant* typological advance.[48] What Covenant Theology tends to miss is the determinate role of the mediatorial head of the covenant. For example, Covenant Theology teaches that the sign of the covenant is applied to the *believer's* offspring rather than to the *mediator's* offspring. Israel circumcised the offspring of Abraham, and the church is to baptize the offspring of Christ.[49] As R. Fowler White writes, "The genealogical principle continues without revocation, but not without reinterpretation under the new covenant."[50] Inclusion within the covenant community can no longer be decided by interpreting the genealogical relationship between the covenant community and the

---

[47] Berkhof, *Systematic Theology*, 633, 634.

[48] Wellum, "Baptism and the Relationship Between the Covenants," 135.

[49] R. Fowler White, "The Last Adam and His Seed: An Exercise in Theological Preemption," *Trinity Journal* 6.1 (Spring 1985), 66, 70, 71.

[50] Ibid., 70.

covenant head in physical terms. The death, resurrection, and ascension of Christ the new covenant Mediator necessitate a spiritual relationship between the covenant community and the covenant head.[51] In other words, Christ has no physical offspring. He has no grandchildren. One becomes "of Christ" through union with Christ, which is appropriated through faith and baptism (Rom 6:4; Gal 3:27-28).

Another important passage in Galatians bearing on the issue of Abraham's offspring isfound in chapter 6:15-16: "For neither circumcision counts for anything, nor uncircumcision, but a new creation. And as for all who walk by this rule, peace and mercy be upon them, and upon the Israel of God." Here, Paul lays down a rule that we can call the "rule of the new creation." In its essence, the rule is that ethnicity does not matter. He then goes on to wish peace and mercy on those who follow this rule of the new creation.

Charles Ryrie writes, "One might also ask why, if the New Testament writers meant to equate clearly Israel and the church, they did not do so plainly in the many other places in their writings where they had convenient opportunity to do so."[52] I think that Paul does just that right here. The issue cannot be solved grammatically, as all agree. The controversy surrounds how one should interpret the "and" (*kai*) in Galatians 6:16. Ryrie thinks the *kai* should be translated "and especially" so Paul is wishing peace and mercy on all who follow this rule that ethnicity does not matter – and especially those Christians who are ethnically Israel. He

---

[51] Ibid., 71; Gentry and Wellum, *Kingdom Through Covenant,* 70, 120-21, 125, 608, 697.

[52] Charles C. Ryrie, *Dispensationalism* (Chicago: Moody, 2007), 149.

writes, "The premillennialist says that Paul is simply singling out Christian Jews for special recognition in the benediction."[53] On the contrary, the *kai* should be understood ep-exegetically (i.e., in an explanatory manner),[54] as the NIV does: "Peace and mercy to all who follow this rule - to the Israel of God."

In light of the argument of the whole book and in light of the immediate context where Paul is clear that ethnicity doesn't matter – I find it incredibly difficult to take "the Israel of God" as referring to anything other than the church, those who are "of Christ" (cf. Gal 3:7, 29). Moises Silva writes, "Since Paul earlier (4:26) had applied Isaiah 54:1 to the Gentile believers in Galatia, and since the letter as a whole focuses on the unity of God's people, it is difficult to believe that at the very end of the document he would introduce an ethnic distinction. Quite the contrary. By means of a final OT allusion the apostle assures his readers that all who belong to the new order, whether Jew or Gentile, are the true seed of Abraham and thus constitute the eschatological Israel of God."[55]

---

[3] Ibid.

[4] Robertson, *The Israel of God*, 42.

[5] Moises Silva, "Galatians," in *Commentary on the New Testament Use of the Old Testament*, eds. G.K. Beale and D.A. Carson (Grand Rapids: Baker Academic, 2007), 810; Similarly, Tom Wright comments, "Those who insist on reading the Galatians passage as if it refers to an exclusively Jewish-Christian group should consider the way in which such an interpretation undoes at a stroke the entire argument of the rest of the letter," in "Jerusalem in the New Testament," 66 n. 22; so also Richard N. Longenecker, *Galatians*, WBC (Dallas: Word, 1990), 298; Bruce W. Longenecker, *The Triumph of Abraham's God*

It should also be pointed out that Paul's benediction of peace and mercy is denied to anyone who allows ethnicity to be a criterion for identifying the people of God![56]

Confirming Evidence:

The inclusion of the nations is obviously anticipated in the Abrahamic covenant itself, as well as other Old Testament passages. Perhaps the most shocking is Isaiah 19:19-25:

> *In that day there will be an altar to the LORD in the midst of the land of Egypt, and a pillar to the LORD at its border. It will be a sign and a witness to the LORD of hosts in the land of Egypt. When they cry to the LORD because of oppressors, he will send them a savior and defender, and deliver them. And the LORD will make himself known to the Egyptians, and the Egyptians will know the LORD in that day and worship with sacrifice and offering, and they will make vows to the LORD and perform them. And the LORD will strike Egypt, striking and healing, and they will return to the LORD, and he will listen to their pleas for mercy and heal them. In that day there will be a highway from Egypt to Assyria, and Assyria will come into Egypt, and Egypt into Assyria, and the Egyptians will worship with the Assyrians. In that day Israel will be the third with Egypt and Assyria, a blessing in the midst of the earth, whom the LORD of hosts has blessed, saying, "Blessed be Egypt my people, and Assyria the work of my hands, and Israel my inheritance."*

Israel will be the third! Egypt my people! Stunning. As O Palmer Robertson notes, "It is almost as though the land o Israel is to be bypassed!"[57]

(Nashville: Abingdon, 1988), 88; LaRondelle, *The Israel of God*, 108-111.

[56] O. Palmer Robertson, *The Israel of God* (Phillipsburg, NJ: P&R, 2000), 4(

[57] Robertson, *The Israel of God*, 21. Christopher Wright writes, "The shock of reading 'Egypt' immediately after 'my people' (instead of the expected Israel) and of putting Israel third on the list is palpable. Yet

The offspring of Abraham experience a "messianic trans-
formation"[58] as one moves from the Abrahamic covenant to
the New Covenant. Here are several other New Testament
passages that are clear in this regard:

John 1:11-12 – *"He came to his own, and his own people did not
receive him. But to all who did receive him, who believed in his name,
he gave the right to become children of God."*

John 8:39 – *"They answered him, 'Abraham is our father.' Jesus
said to them, 'If you were Abraham's children, you would be doing
the works Abraham did'."*

Romans 2:28-29 - *"For no one is a Jew who is merely one out-
wardly, nor is circumcision outward and physical. But a Jew is one
inwardly, and circumcision is a matter of the heart, by the Spirit, not
by the letter. His praise is not from man but from God."*

Romans 4:11-12 - *"He received the sign of circumcision as a seal
of the righteousness that he had by faith while he was still uncircum-
cised. The purpose was to make him the father of all who believe without being circumcised, so that righteousness would be counted to
them as well, and to make him the father of the circumcised who are
not merely circumcised but who also walk in the footsteps of the faith
that our father Abraham had before he was circumcised."*

Romans 4:16 - *"That is why it depends on faith, in order that the
promise may rest on grace and be guaranteed to all his offspring--not
only to the adherent of the law but also to the one who shares the faith
of Abraham, who is the father of us all."*

1 Corinthians 10:1 - *"For I want you to know, brothers, that our
fathers were all under the cloud, and all passed through the sea."*

---

there it is. The archenemies of Israel will be absorbed into the identity, titles and privileges of Israel and share in the Abrahamic blessing
of the living God, YHWH," in *The Mission of God,* 493.

[58] David G. Peterson, *Transformed by God* (Downers Gove, IL: IVP Academic, 2012), 101.

Philippians 3:2-3 - *"Look out for the dogs, look out for the evildo-ers, look out for those who mutilate the flesh. For we are the circumci-sion, who worship by the Spirit of God and glory in Christ Jesus and put no confidence in the flesh."*

Ephesians 2:13-16 - *"But now in Christ Jesus you who once were far away have been brought near by the blood of Christ. For he himself is our peace, who has made the two groups one and has destroyed the barrier, the dividing wall of hostility, by setting aside in his flesh the law with its commands and regulations. His purpose was to create in himself one new humanity out of the two, thus making peace, and in one body to reconcile both of them to God through the cross, by which he put to death their hostility."* (NIV)

Hays writes, "The church discovers its true identity only in relation to the sacred story of Israel, and the sacred story of Israel discovers its full significance – so Paul passionately believed – only in relation to God's unfolding design for salvation of the Gentiles in the church."[59]

---

[59] Hays, *Echoes of Scripture in the Letters of Paul,* 100-01; James W. Aageson, *Written Also for Our Sake: Paul and the Art of Biblical Interpreta-tion* (Louisville: Westminster/John Knox Press, 1993), 84.

Chapter 5:
Blessing

Blessing is an important theme in Genesis. Notice the fivefold repetition of the Hebrew root for the word "to bless" (*brk*) in 12:2-3: "And I will make of you a great nation, and I will *bless* you and make your name great, so that you will be a *blessing*. I will *bless* those who *bless* you, and him who dishonors you I will curse, and in you all the families of the earth shall be *blessed*" (italics mine).[60] Blessing restores all the good that God has given mankind in the beginning.[61] Richard Bauckham writes, "Blessing is a rich biblical notion that has been rather neglected in Christian theology. Blessing in the Bible refers to God's characteristically generous and abundant giving of all good to his creatures and his continual renewal of the abundance of created life. Blessing is God's provision for human flourishing."[62]

Blessing reverses the curses of Genesis 3. There God says there will be conflict between the seed of the serpent and the seed of the woman, conflict between the woman and the man, and conflict between the man and the ground. The conflict between the man and woman is addressed in the promise of a great nation. The conflict between the man and

---

[60] Alexander, *From Paradise to the Promised Land*, 146. Gentry and Wellum, *Kingdom Through Covenant*, 242.

[61] Goheen, *A Light to the Nations*, 31; Wright, *The Mission of God*, 209.

[62] Richard Bauckham, *Bible and Mission* (Grand Rapids: Baker Academic, 2005), 34.

the ground is addressed by the promise of the land to be given to Abraham's offspring. The conflict between the off-spring of the woman and the offspring of the serpent is ad-dressed by the promise of blessing for those who bless Abraham and cursing for those who curse him.[63]

The essence of this blessing is a special relationship with God. This was God's original creational intent and this was what Adam and Eve lost. Adam and Eve were in God's spe-cial presence, but after the catastrophe, the place that they were to protect has to be protected from them (Gen 3:23-24)![64] The covenant with Abraham will right this wrong. Genesis 17:7-8 reads, "And I will establish my covenant be-tween me and you and your offspring after you throughout their generations for an everlasting covenant, to be God to you and to your offspring after you. And I will give to you and to your offspring after you the land of your sojournings, all the land of Canaan, for an everlasting possession, and I will be their God." Here we have the covenant formula laced throughout the Canon: I will be your God and you will be my people.[65]

If we are sinners and God is holy, how can we enjoy this blessing of a special relationship with our Creator? We learn the answer in Galatians 3:8-9: "And the Scripture, foreseeing that God would justify the Gentiles by faith, preached the gospel beforehand to Abraham, saying, "In you shall all the

---

[63] James Hamilton, "The Seed of the Woman and the Blessing of Abra-ham," Tyndale Bulletin 58.2 (2007), 260-61.

[64] Sandra L. Richter, *The Epic of Eden: A Christian Entry into the Old Testa-ment* (Downers Grove, IL: IVP Academic, 2008), 112, 159.

[65] David Baker, *Two Testaments, One Bible* (Downers Grove, IL: IVP Aca-demic, 2010), 242-43.

nations be blessed." So then, those who are of faith are blessed along with Abraham, the man of faith." In Galatians 3:8, Paul merges Genesis 12:3 and 18:18:[66]

> Genesis 12:3 – *"I will bless those who bless you, and him who dishonors you I will curse, and in you all the families of the earth shall be blessed."*

> Genesis 18:18 - *"seeing that Abraham shall surely become a great and mighty nation, and all the nations of the earth shall be blessed in him?"*

Notice how Paul personifies the Bible.[67] Scripture foresaw. The gospel was proclaimed to Abraham and that gospel is defined here as justification by faith for the Gentiles. The blessing of the nations is forgiveness (Rom 4:4-12). As John Reisinger writes, "The true blessing of Abraham is nothing less than justification by faith."[68] The blessing of Abraham is *sola fide* for the nations. Abraham is the model here, contrary to Jewish tradition:[69]

> "He kept the law of the Most High, and entered into covenant with him" (Sirach 44:20)

---

[66] Schreiner, *Galatians*, 194.

[67] What Scripture says, God says. See Benjamin B. Warfield, "It Says:" "Scripture Says:" "God Says," *The Presbyterian and Reformed Review*, (1899), 472.

[68] John G. Reisinger, *Abraham's Four Seeds: A Biblical Examination of the Presuppositions of Covenant Theology and Dispensationalism* (Frederick, MD: New Covenant Media), 39.

[69] John Barclay writes, "On the basis of Gen 26:5 ('Abraham obeyed my voice and kept my charge, my commandments, my statutes and my laws') and similar verses concerning Abraham's obedience, it was assumed in Jewish traditions of many kinds that Abraham had kept the law even before its promulgation on Sinai," *Obeying the Truth* (Vancouver: Regent College Publishing, 1988), 66.

"Was not Abraham found faithful when tested, and it was reckoned to him as righteousness?" (1 Macc 2:52)

Paul reads Genesis 12 in light of Genesis 15 (cf. Rom 4:9, 21, 22).[70] All the nations of the earth will be blessed through Abraham. How? By being counted righteous through faith, just like Abraham.

Galatians 3:14

Galatians 3:14 also speaks of the blessing of Abraham: "so that in Christ Jesus the blessing of Abraham might come to the Gentiles, so that we might receive the promised Spirit through faith." Here the two purpose clauses are coordinate and mutually interpret one another.[71] Here Paul defines the blessing of Abraham as the Holy Spirit.

How can Paul say this? I do not recall the Holy Spirit being mentioned in Genesis 12 and following, do you? Many hermeneutical systems have no room for what the Holy Spirit – through Paul – does here. The original context – narrowly defined - does not exhaust its meaning. There is a "fuller sense" that God knew all along but isn't understood by us fully until God makes it clearer through progressive revelation.[72] We must be *canonical* exegetes, interpreting the

---

[70] Schreiner, *Galatians,* 194.

[71] Schreiner, *Paul,* 78; idem., *Galatians,* 218. Dumbrell, "Abraham and the Abrahamic Covenant in Galatians 3:1-14," 27.

[72] Peter Enns, "Fuller Meaning, Single Goal: A Christotelic Approach to the New Testament Use of the Old in Its First-Century Interpretive Environment," in *Three Views on the New Testament Use of the Old Testament* eds. Kenneth Berding and Jonathan Lunde (Grand Rapids: Zondervan, 2007), 205; Douglas Moo, "The Problem of Sensus Plenior," in *Hermeneutics, Authority, and Canon* eds. D.A. Carson and John D. Woodbridge (Grand Rapids: Zondervan, 1986); Gentry and Wellum, *Kingdom Through Covenant,* 117 n.82.

former revelation in light of the latter. If the "grammatical-historical" method of exegesis excludes or ignores the re-demptive-historical setting of the fulfillment of God's pur-poses in Christ, then we need to jettison or at least adjust our hermeneutic.[73] Dennis Johnson writes, "When any herme-neutic method disqualifies – or seems to disqualify, by pit-ting an Old Testament text's 'original' meaning against its interpretation in the New – the ways that Jesus, the Word of God incarnate, interpreted the Word of God written and taught his apostles to do so, this dissonance is a signal that something is seriously amiss."[74]

---

[73] Johnson, *Him We Proclaim,* 151-64. Gentry and Wellum write, "Gram-matical-historical exegesis needs to be set in the larger context of a canonical reading of Scripture; the parts must be read in terms of the whole," Gentry and Wellum, *Kingdom Through Covenant,* 86. I do not understand how Craig Blaising and Darrell Bock can assert "No claim is ever made by Paul that God has discarded the promises, re-formulated, or resignified them." *Progressive Dispensationalism,* 270. God has certainly not discarded the promises but as we see here and as we will see in the section on land, they have certainly been refor-mulated and expanded in light of the coming of Christ and the Spirit.

[74] Ibid., 153. G.K. Beale notes, "The usual 'strict' understanding of a 'grammatical-historical' approach is too limited in its scope, since it studies a passage primarily from only two angles: (1) investigation of only the human author's viewpoint through a study of the historical, linguistic, grammatical, genre contexts, etc., of a passage; (2) the di-vine author can theoretically be left out of consideration until the 'grammatical-historical' study is complete, since the meaning sought for is only that of the human author. For example, even an interpreter who does not believe in divine inspiration must study a prophet like Isaiah from the viewpoint that Isaiah himself believed that he was in-spired in what he wrote, and, therefore, that intention must be pro-jected onto the process of interpreting Isaiah. How much more should this be the case for the believing exegete? Accordingly, this is

In my view, Paul interprets Genesis 12 in light of its broader, canonical context.[75] He reads the Abrahamic promises in light of the whole Old Testament storyline.[76] He doesn't even feel the need to prove this point or spell it out. Presumably, he has already done so and now can simply assert it.[77] Anyone familiar with their Hebrew Bible would not be shocked by this statement though. Consider a handful of the many promises about the coming of the Spirit:

> Ezekiel 11:19-20 - *"And I will give them one heart, and a new spirit I will put within them. I will remove the heart of stone from their flesh and give them a heart of flesh, that they may walk in my*

---

only one example showing that considering divine intention should be part of a grammatical-historical approach. Thus, grammatical-historical exegesis and typology are two aspects of the same thing: hearing God speak in Scripture." "The Use of Hosea 11:1 in Matthew 2:15: One More Time," *JETS* 55, no. 4 (2012): 700 n. 14.

[75] Kevin J. Vanhoozer, *Is There A Meaning in This Text?* (Grand Rapids: Baker, 1998), 265. Contra Walter Kaiser, who writes, "It is a mark of *eis*egesis, not *ex*egesis, to borrow freight that appears chronologically later in the text and to transport it back and unload it on an earlier passage simply because both or all the passages involved share the same Canon," in *Toward an Exegetical Theology* (Grand Rapids: Baker, 1981), 82.

[76] On the eschatological significance of the gift of the Spirit, see Anthony Hoekema, *The Bible and the Future* (Grand Rapids: Eerdmans, 1979), 55-67. Geerhardus Vos writes, "The 'Pneuma' was in the mind of the Apostle before all else the element of the eschatological or the celestial sphere, that which characterizes the mode of existence and life in the world to come and consequently of that anticipated form in which the world to come is even now realized in heaven," in *The Pauline Eschatology* (Phillipsburg, NJ: P&R Publishing, 1994), 59.

[77] Contra Hays, *Echoes of Scripture in the Letters of Paul,* 110 who thinks there is no textual warrant and that Paul is merely talking about their experience of the Spirit mentioned in 3:1-5.

statutes and keep my rules and obey them. And they shall be my people, and I will be their God."

Ezekiel 36:26-27 - "And I will give you a new heart, and a new spirit I will put within you. And I will remove the heart of stone from your flesh and give you a heart of flesh. And I will put my Spirit within you, and cause you to walk in my statutes and be careful to obey my rules."

Ezekiel 37:14 - "And I will put my Spirit within you, and you shall live, and I will place you in your own land. Then you shall know that I am the LORD; I have spoken, and I will do it, declares the LORD."

Ezekiel 39:29 - "And I will not hide my face anymore from them, when I pour out my Spirit upon the house of Israel, declares the Lord GOD."

Isaiah 11:1-2 – "There shall come forth a shoot from the stump of Jesse, and a branch from his roots shall bear fruit. And the Spirit of the LORD shall rest upon him, the Spirit of wisdom and understanding, the Spirit of counsel and might, the Spirit of knowledge and the fear of the LORD" (cf. Isa 4:2-6).

Isaiah 32:15 - "until the Spirit is poured upon us from on high, and the wilderness becomes a fruitful field, and the fruitful field is deemed a forest."

Isaiah 42:1 - "Behold my servant, whom I uphold, my chosen, in whom my soul delights; I have put my Spirit upon him; he will bring forth justice to the nations."

Isaiah 44:3 - "For I will pour water on the thirsty land, and streams on the dry ground; I will pour my Spirit upon your offspring, and my blessing on your descendants."[78]

---

[78] The text Paul probably specifically has in mind is Isaiah 44:3, since it mentions both blessing and the Spirit. See Schreiner, *Galatians,* 221; Don Garlington, *An Exposition of Galatians* (Eugene, OR: Wipf and Stock, 2007), 207.

Isaiah 61:1 - *"The Spirit of the Lord GOD is upon me, because the LORD has anointed me to bring good news to the poor; he has sent me to bind up the brokenhearted, to proclaim liberty to the captives, and the opening of the prison to those who are bound"* (cf. Acts 2:33).

Isaiah 63:11 - *"Then he remembered the days of old, of Moses and his people. Where is he who brought them up out of the sea with the shepherds of his flock? Where is he who put in the midst of them his Holy Spirit?"*

Joel 2:28-29 - *"And it shall come to pass afterward, that I will pour out my Spirit on all flesh; your sons and your daughters shall prophesy, your old men shall dream dreams, and your young men shall see visions. Even on the male and female servants in those days I will pour out my Spirit"*

The Holy Spirit was only poured out on select individuals for a limited period of time in the Old Covenant, but that would all change with the coming of the New Covenant. Moses had said, "Are you jealous for my sake? Would that all the LORD's people were prophets, that the LORD would put his Spirit on them" (Num 11:29). This would indeed be the case at Pentecost and beyond. The age to come would be the age of the universal outpouring of the Spirit.

Paul began his letter with this same idea: Jesus "gave himself for our sins to deliver us from the present evil age" (Gal 1:4). Anthony Hoekema writes, "the reception of the Spirit means that one has become a participant in the new mode of existence associated with the future age, and now partakes of the 'powers of the age to come'."[79] Their experi-

---

[79] Anthony A. Hoekema, *The Bible and the Future* (Grand Rapids: Eerdmans, 1979), 58; Geerhardus Vos, "Eschatology and the Spirit in Paul" in *Biblical and Theological Studies by the Members of the Faculty of*

ence of the Spirit (Gal 3:1-5) is a sign that God's eschatological restoration of Israel has begun. The Spirit is the way the promised blessing made to Abraham is being realized in all of Abraham's true children.[80]

This is why the Spirit is referred to as the "guarantee of our inheritance" (Eph 1:14; 2 Cor 1:22, 5:5) of the world to come.[81] The gift of the Spirit is the first fruits of the eschatological harvest. The first fruits stand for the beginning of the harvest; it is an experience in part of the harvest now and a pledge of more of the same kind and quality to come (Rom 8:23). The coming of the Spirit means the age to come is here.[82] The Abrahamic covenant finds its fulfillment in the new covenant and the gift of the Spirit is at the heart of the new covenant.

Princeton Theological Seminary (Birmingham, AL: Solid Ground Books, 2003), 258-59.

[80] Gordon D. Fee, *God's Empowering Presence* (Peabody, MA: Hendrickson, 1994), 394-95.

[81] Michael F. Bird, *Introducing Paul* (Downers Grove, IL: IVP Academic, 2008), 47.

[82] The Pauline contrast of flesh and Spirit is undergirded by the contrast between the old and new age. As Herman Ridderbos writes, "Flesh (body) and Spirit do not stand over against one another here as two 'parts' in the human existence or in the existence of Christ.... Rather, 'flesh' and 'Spirit' represent two modes of existence, on the one hand that of the old aeon which is characterized and determined by the flesh, on the other that of the new creation which is of the Spirit of God," in Herman Ridderbos, *Paul: An Outline of His Theology* (Grand Rapids: Eerdmans, 1966), 66.

Chapter 6:
Land

As mentioned above, I take 2 Corinthians 1:20 *literally:* "For no matter how many promises God has made, they are 'Yes' in Christ" (NIV). I also assume that the "land promise" is included in "no matter how many promises God has made."

It is important to continually point out that land is not new in the Abrahamic covenant. Land was important before Genesis 12; in fact, it is important from the first page of the Bible. As O. Palmer Robertson writes, "The original idea of land as paradise significantly shaped the expectations associated with redemption. As the place of blessedness arising from unbroken fellowship and communion with God, the land of paradise became the goal toward which redeemed humanity was returning."[83] Creation points forward to the new creation. Furthermore, the Creator God's choice of one particular portion of the earth in which to focus on naturally leads to the expectation that through this one people all the nations of the earth will be blessed.[84] Behind the promise of a particular piece of land in the Abraham narrative stood

---

[83] Robertson, *The Israel of God*, 4; Gentry and Wellum, *Kingdom Through Covenant*, 709.

[84] Ibid., 9. Robertson also points out that Israel was a narrow land bridge connecting Africa, Europe, and Asia and therefore was perfectly situated for the extension of God's blessing to the nations, Robertson, *The Israel of God*, 11.

God's prior promise to use the people of that land as a means to bless all the nations of the earth.

Shockingly, when discussing Abraham in Galatians 3, Paul omits the land! W.D. Davies suggests that his silence points not to the absence of conscious concern with it, but to his deliberate rejection of it.[85] Paul also frequently uses the language of "promise" with no mention of land (cf. 2 Cor 7:1; Eph 1:13, 2:12, 3:6; Rom 15:8-9).[86]

When Paul does bring up the land, he universalizes it; Romans 4:13 says that the promise to Abraham is that he would be heir of the world (*kosmos*). Ephesians 6:2-3 says that children should honor their parents "that it may go well with you and that you may live long in the land." In alluding to Exodus 20:12, Paul omits "that the Lord your God is giving you." Here, clearly, the theme of land has been expanded to include the whole world.[87]

There is no reference to the word "land" in Galatians, but when dealing with this issue, one must consider other words like "Jerusalem," "temple," "mountain," "Zion," and "throne" as well. Galatians does not mention "land," but there is a reference to "Jerusalem" and "Mount" in chapter 4. There, Paul does not portray a very positive view of Jerusalem's future. The Judaizers probably used the narrative in Genesis 21 to say that Gentiles are of Ishmael and must be

---

[85] W.D. Davies, *The Gospel and the Land* (Los Angeles: The University of California Press, 1974), 179.

[86] P.W.L. Walker, *Jesus and the Holy City*, 117.

[87] Robertson, *The Israel of God*, 28.

circumcised to be true children of promise.[88] Here Paul uses "hermeneutical jujitsu."[89] Galatians 4:21-31 reads,

> Tell me, you who desire to be under the law, do you not listen to the law? For it is written that Abraham had two sons, one by a slave woman and one by a free woman. But the son of the slave was born according to the flesh, while the son of the free woman was born through promise. Now this may be interpreted allegorically: these women are two covenants. One is from Mount Sinai, bearing children for slavery; she is Hagar. Now Hagar is Mount Sinai in Arabia; she corresponds to the present Jerusalem, for she is in slavery with her children. But the Jerusalem above is free, and she is our mother. For it is written, "Rejoice, O barren one who does not bear; break forth and cry aloud, you who are not in labor! For the children of the desolate one will be more than those of the one who has a husband." Now you, brothers, like Isaac, are children of promise. But just as at that time he who was born according to the flesh persecuted him who was born according to the Spirit, so also it is now. But what does the Scripture say? "Cast out the slave woman and her son, for the son of the slave woman shall not inherit with the son of the free woman." So, brothers, we are not children of the slave but of the free woman.

Let me summarize: Abraham had two sons: Isaac and Ishmael. Isaac is of the free woman and was born through promise. Ishmael is a son of the slave woman and was born according to the flesh (i.e., human effort). These women are two covenants, which are the old and the new covenants.[90]

---

[88] Longenecker, *Galatians,* 210; David G. Peterson, *Transformed by God: New Covenant Life and Ministry* (Downers Grove, IL: IVP Academic, 2012), 133.

[89] Hays, *Echoes of Scripture in the Letters of Paul,* 112.

[90] The majority of commentators take this view. E.g., See Longenecker, *Galatians,* 211; Schreiner, *Galatians,* 269; Fee, *God's Empowering Presence,* 413, 416. Contra Hays, *Echoes of Scripture in the Letters of Paul,* 114-15 who opts for the Abrahamic and Old covenants.

Hagar is Mount Sinai, bearing children of slavery. She is the present Jerusalem. "Present" Jerusalem takes us back to the earlier reference to the "present" evil age (Gal 1:4).[91]. The present Jerusalem and her children are in slavery. Her children (4:25) are those who are dependent on her. She is no longer our mother. Our mother is the Jerusalem above, and she is free. To say that the Jerusalem above is our mother is to say we belong to the new age. We are the children of the new creation – the Judaizers are of the old creation. We are the people of the new age, the children of promise (4:28). Tom Schreiner writes, "The Jerusalem above, according to Paul, is the eschatological Jerusalem that has reached down into the present evil age, so we have an example here of Paul's already but not yet eschatology."[92] The Judaizers claimed Abraham for their father and Jerusalem for their mother, and Paul says that Christian identity is bound to Christ and the Jerusalem above.[93]

To substantiate his claim, Paul quotes Isaiah 54, which is about the restoration of Jerusalem and Israel (54:5-7). This is significant, as it follows on the heels of the story of the Suffering Servant.[94] How could the covenant be fulfilled if this Servant is "cut off" and "struck" (Isa 53:8)? The "many children" of Isaiah 54:1 are to be found in the Gentile churches – the spiritual Zion. The offspring of the Servant will not be physical offspring, but spiritual! The new people of God are not defined by circumcised foreskin but circumcised hearts

---

[91] Meyer, *The End of the Law* 129.

[92] Schreiner, *Galatians,* 272.

[93] P.W.L. Walker, *Jesus and the Holy City* (Grand Rapids: Eerdmans, 1996), 129-30.

[94] See White, "The Last Adam and His Seed," 70-72.

(Deut 30:6). Through Christ, the forsaken suf⟨ "many" will be justified; Jesus "will see His ⟨ 11); God is restoring his people.

Jerusalem was a type pointing forward to the New Jerusa-lem, the church. This is similar to the theology of the author of Hebrews: "But you have come to Mount Zion and to the city of the living God, the heavenly Jerusalem, and to innu-merable angels in festal gathering, and to the assembly of the firstborn who are enrolled in heaven, and to God, the judge of all, and to the spirits of the righteous made perfect, and to Jesus, the mediator of a new covenant, and to the sprinkled blood that speaks a better word than the blood of Abel" (12:22-24).[95] John similarly writes about the new Jeru-salem and what is often missed is that it is a people – not a place. The new Jerusalem is the bride of Christ: "And I saw the holy city, new Jerusalem, coming down out of heaven from God, prepared as a bride adorned for her husband" (Rev 21:2). John explicitly contrasts this bride with the pros-titute of chapter 17, which I take to be apostate Jerusalem:

> "Then one of the seven angels who had the seven bowls came and said to me, "Come, I will show you the judgment of the great prosti-tute who is seated on many waters... And he carried me away in the Spirit into a wilderness, and I saw a woman sitting on a scarlet beast that was full of blasphemous names, and it had seven heads and ten horns" (17:1, 3).

> "Then came one of the seven angels who had the seven bowls full of the seven last plagues and spoke to me, saying, "Come, I will show you the Bride, the wife of the Lamb." And he carried me away in the

---

[95] Peter Walker, "Jerusalem in Hebrews 13:9-14 and the Dating of the Epistle," *Tyndale Bulletin* 45.1 (1994), 44-49.

Spirit to a great, high mountain, and showed me the holy city Jerusalem coming down out of heaven from God" (21:9-10).

So the promise of land pointed beyond itself. The promise of land was temporary[96] and typological.[97] Tom Wright notes, "The Land, like the Torah, was a temporary stage in the long purpose of the God of Abraham. It was not a bad thing now done away with, but a good and necessary thing now fulfilled in Christ and the Spirit. It is as though the Land were a great advance metaphor for the design of God that his people should eventually bring the whole world into submission to his healing reign. God's whole purpose now goes beyond Jerusalem and the Land to the whole world."[98]

It seems to me that Dispensational leader Charles Ryrie completely misses this clear New Testament teaching when he writes, "If the yet unfulfilled prophecies of the Old Testament made in the Abrahamic, Davidic, and new covenants

---

[96] Donaldson, "The Kingdom of God and the Land," in *The Gospel and the Land of Promise,* 67.

[97] As Meredith Kline puts it, "In the New Testament there are clear indications of a positive kind of the shift to the second level of meaning of the land promise. Indeed, with surprising abruptness the New Testament disregards the first level meaning [i.e., Israel's possession of Canaan] and simply takes for granted that the second level, cosmic fulfillment is the true intention of the promise," in *Kingdom Prologue* (Eugene, OR: Wipf and Stock, 2006), 339.

[98] Tom Wright, "Jerusalem in the New Testament," in *Jerusalem Past and Present in the Purposes of God,* ed. P.W.L. Walker (Cambridge: Tyndale House, 1992) 67. Bruce Waltke argues that "the New Testament redefines Land in three ways: first, *spiritually,* as a reference to Christ's person; second, *transcendentally,* as a reference to heavenly Jerusalem; and third, *eschatologically,* as a reference to the new Jerusalem after Christ's second coming." *An Old Testament Theology* (Grand Rapids: Zondervan, 2007), 560.

are to be literally fulfilled, there must be a future period, the Millennium, in which they can be fulfilled, for the church is not now fulfilling them."[99] The promise land was a type of the whole world.

Christopher Wright gives the following helpful illustration:

> Imagine a father who, in the days before mechanized transport, promises his son, aged 5, that when he is 21 he will give him a horse for himself. Meanwhile the motor car is invented. So on his 21st birthday the son awakes to find a motor car outside, 'with love from Dad.' It would be a strange son who would accuse his father of breaking his promise just because there was no horse. And even stranger if, in spite of having received the far superior motor car, the son insisted that the promise would only be fulfilled if a horse *also* materialized, since that was the literal promise. It is obvious that with the change in circumstances, unknown at the time the promise was made, the father has more than kept his promise. In fact he has done so in a way that *surpasses* the original words of the promise which were necessarily limited by the mode of transport available at that time. The promise was made in terms understood at the time. It was fulfilled in the light of new historical events.[100]

---

[99] Ryrie, *Dispensationalism,* 172.

[100] Christopher J.H. Wright, *Knowing Jesus Through the Old Testament* (Downers Grove, IL: IVP Academic, 1992), 71. G.K. Beale applies the same analogy in *The Temple and the Church's Mission* (Downers Grove, IL: IVP, 2004), 291. O. Palmer Robertson writes, "In the nature of things, these writers could only employ images with which they and their hearers were familiar. So they spoke of a return to the geographical land of Israel. Indeed there was a return to this land, though hardly on the scale prophesied by Ezekiel. But in the context of the realities of the new covenant, this land must be understood in terms

The kingdom of God takes over from and fulfills the land motif of the Old Testament, and extends it to its fullest potential and promise.[101] The land has been "Christified." To be "in Christ" has replaced being "in the Land." Being "in Christ" frees us from the Law, and therefore from the land.[102]

---

of the newly recreated cosmos about which the apostle Paul speaks in Romans. The whole universe (which is 'the land' from a new covenant perspective) groans in travail, waiting for the redemption that will come with the resurrection of the bodies of the redeemed (Rom. 8:22-23). The return to paradise in the framework of the new covenant does not involve merely a return to the shadowy forms of the old covenant. It means the rejuvenation of the entire earth. By this renewal of the entire creation, the old covenant's promise of land finds its new covenant realization," *The Israel of God,* 26.

[101] Alistair Donaldson, "The Kingdom of God and the Land," in *The Gospel and the Land of Promise,* eds. Philip Church, Peter Walker, Tim Bulkeley, and Tim Meadowcroft, (Eugene, OR: Pickwick, 2011), 74.

[102] LaRondelle, *The Israel of God,* 142.

Conclusion

In sum, Abraham was promised numerous offspring and they continue to increase, we are blessed with being declared right through faith, we are blessed with the gift of the Spirit who guarantees us that God's future is here and there is yet more to come, and the Jerusalem above is our Mother. I hope this little exercise has helped you have further confirmation that all the promises of God are yes and amen in Christ (2 Cor 1:20)!

Bibliography

Aageson, James W. *Written Also for Our Sake: Paul and the Art of Biblical Interpretation.* Louisville: Westminster/John Knox Press, 1993.

Alexander, T. Desmond. *From Paradise to the Promised Land.* Grand Rapids: Baker Academic, 2002.

Baker, David. *Two Testaments, One Bible.* Downers Grove, IL: IVP Academic, 2010.

Barclay, John. *Obeying the Truth.* Vancouver: Regent College Publishing, 1988.

Bauckham, Richard. *Bible and Mission.* Grand Rapids: Baker Academic, 2005.

Beale, G.K. *The Temple and the Church's Mission.* NSBT. Downers Grove, IL: IVP, 2004.

Berkhof, Louis. *Systematic Theology.* Grand Rapids: Eerdmans, 1996.

Bird, Michael. *Introducing Paul.* Downers Grove, IL: IVP Academic, 2008.

Blaising, Craig A. and Darrell L. Bock. *Progressive Dispensationalism.* Grand Rapids: Baker Books, 1993.

Davies, W.D. *The Gospel and the Land.* Los Angeles: The University of California Press, 1974.

Dempster, Stephen G. *Dominion and Dynasty: A Theology of the Hebrew Bible.* NSBT Downers Grove, IL: IVP, 2003.

Diffey, Daniel S. "The Royal Promise in Genesis: The Often Underestimated Importance of Genesis 17:6, 17:16, and 35:11." *Tyndale Bulletin* 62, no. 2 (2011).

Donaldson, Alistair. "The Kingdom of God and the Land." In *The Gospel and the Land of Promise.* Edited by Philip Church, Peter Walker, Tim Bulkeley, and Tim Meadowcroft. Eugene, OR: Pickwick, 2011.

Dumbrell, William J. *The Search for Order.* Eugene, OR: Wipf & Stock, 1994.

_____. "Abraham and the Abrahamic Covenant in Galatians 3:1-14." In *The Gospel to the Nations: Paul's Mission.* Edited by Peter Bolt and Mark Thompson. Downers Grove, IL: IVP, 2000.

_____. *Covenant and Creation.* Carlisle, PA: Paternoster, 1984.

_____. "The Covenant with Abraham." *The Reformed Theological Review* 2, no. 41 (May-August 1982).

Ellis, E. Earl. *Paul's Use of the Old Testament.* Eugene, OR: Wiph and Stock, 1981.

Enns, Peter. "Fuller Meaning, Single Goal: A Christotelic Approach to the New Testament Use of the Old in Its First Century Interpretive Environment." In *Three Views on the New Testament Use of the Old Testament.* Edited by Kenneth Berding and Jonathan Lunde. Grand Rapids:

Zondervan, 2007.

Fee, Gordon D. *God's Empowering Presence.* Peabody, MA: Hendrickson, 1994.

Garlington, Don. *An Exposition of Galatians.* Eugene, OR: Wipf and Stock, 2007.

Gentry, Peter J. and Stephen J. Wellum. *Kingdom Through Covenant: A Biblical-Theological Understanding of the Covenants.* Wheaton, IL: Crossway, 2012.

Goheen, Michael W. *A Light to the Nations.* Grand Rapids: Baker, 2011.

Goldsworthy, Graeme. *Gospel-Centered Hermeneutics.* Downers Grove, IL: IVP Academic, 2006.

Hamilton, James. "The Seed of the Woman and the Blessing of Abraham." *Tyndale Bulletin* 58, no. 2 (2007).

Hays, Richard B. *Echoes of Scripture in the Letters of Paul.* London: Yale University Press, 1989.

_____. "The Canonical Matrix of the Gospels." In *The Cambridge Companion to the Gospels.* Edited by Stephen C. Barton. Cambridge: Cambridge University Press, 2006.

Hoekema, Anthony A. *The Bible and the Future.* Grand Rapids: Eerdmans, 1979.

Johnson, Dennis E. *Him We Proclaim.* Phillipsburg, NJ: P&R, 2007.

Kirk, J.R. Daniel. *Jesus Have I Loved, but Paul?* Grand Rapids: Baker Academic, 2011.

Kline, Meredith. *Kingdom Prologue.* Eugene, OR: Wipf and Stock, 2006.

Köstenberger, Andreas and Peter T. O'Brien. *Salvation to the Ends of the Earth.* NSBT. Downers Grove, IL: IVP, 2001.

LaRondelle, Hans K. *The Israel of God in Prophecy.* Berrien Springs, MI: Andrews University Press, 1983.

Longenecker, Bruce W. *The Triumph of Abraham's God.* Nashville: Abingdon, 1988.

Longenecker, Richard N. *Galatians.* Word Biblical Commentary. Dallas: Word, 1990.

Moore, Russell. "Personal and Cosmic Eschatology." In *A Theology for the Church.* Edited by Daniel L. Akin. Nashville: B&H Academic, 2007.

Peterson, David G. *Transformed by God.* Downers Grove, IL: IVP Academic, 2012.

Reisinger, John. *Abraham's Four Seeds.* Frederick, MD: New Covenant Media, 1998.

Richter, Sandra L. *The Epic of Eden: A Christian Entry into the Old Testament.* Downers Grove, IL: IVP Academic, 2008.

Ridderbos, Herman. *Paul: An Outline of His Theology.* Grand Rapids: Eerdmans, 1966.

Robertson, O. Palmer. *The Israel of God*. Phillipsburg, NJ: P&R, 2000.

Ryrie, Charles C. *Dispensationalism*. Chicago: Moody, 2007.

Schreiner, Thomas R. *Galatians*. Zondervan Exegetical Commentary. Grand Rapids: Zondervan, 2010.

Silva, Moises. "Galatians." In *Commentary on the New Testament Use of the Old Testament*. Edited by G.K. Beale and D.A. Carson. Grand Rapids: Baker Academic, 2007.

Vanhoozer, Kevin J. *Is There a Meaning in This Text?* Grand Rapids: Baker, 1998.

Vos, Geerhardus. "Eschatology and the Spirit in Paul." In *Biblical and Theological Studies by the Members of the Faculty of Princeton Theological Seminary*. Birmingham, AL: Solid Ground Books, 2003.

_____. *The Pauline Eschatology*. Phillipsburg, NJ: P&R, 1994.

Walker, P.W.L. "Jerusalem in Hebrews 13:9-14 and the Dating of the Epistle." *Tyndale Bulletin* 45, no. 1 (1994).

_____. *Jesus and the Holy City*. Grand Rapids: Eerdmans, 1996.

Wellum, Stephen J. "Baptism and the Relationship between the Covenants." In *Believer's Baptism: Sign of the New Covenant in Christ*. Edited by Thomas R. Schreiner and Shawn D. Wright. Nashville: B&H Academic, 2006.

White, A. Blake. *Union With Christ: Last Adam and Seed of Abraham.* Frederick, MD: New Covenant Media, 2012.

White, R. Fowler. "The Last Adam and His Seed: An Exercise in Theological Preemption." *Trinity Journal* 6, no. 1 (Spring 1985).

Williamson, Paul R. *Sealed With an Oath.* NSBT. Downers Grove, IL: IVP, 2007.

Wright, Christopher J.H. *Knowing Jesus Through the Old Testament.* Downers Grove, IVP Academic, 1992.

_____. *The Mission of God.* Downers Grove, IL: IVP Academic, 2006.

Wright, N.T. "Jerusalem in the New Testament." In *Jerusalem Past and Present in the Purposes of God.* Edited by P.W.L. Walker. Cambridge: Tyndale House, 1992.

_____. *Justification.* Downers, Grove, IL: IVP Academic, 2009.

_____. *The New Testament and the People of God.* Minneapolis: Fortress, 1992.

Made in the USA
Charleston, SC
06 September 2013